Signature Page

To

_____

"Because I see greatness in you"

From

[signature]
_____

Author Signature
[signature]
_____

greatness

DAVID L. COOK, PH.D.

Copyright© 2021 David L. Cook, Ph.D.
All rights reserved including the right to reproduce this book
or portions thereof in any form.

ISBN 978-0-9818051-2-2

Printed by Walsworth Publishing Company, Inc. Marceline MO.

CONTENTS

References. vii
Acknowledgments. xi
Foreword by Ken Blanchard xiii
Introduction xvii

CHAPTER 1: The Greatest Predictor of Success. 1

Pillar I: Focus: "Where do you want to go?" 7

CHAPTER 2: Twenty Minutes Before the Trophy Celebration. 9
CHAPTER 3: Specific Goals. 17
CHAPTER 4: Tangible Goals 21
CHAPTER 5: Difficult Goals. 25
CHAPTER 6: Self-Referenced Goals 29

Pillar II: Passion: "How bad do you want to reach your goal?" 33

CHAPTER 7: The Fuel of Passion. 35
CHAPTER 8: Ownership. 37
CHAPTER 9: Accountability. 41
CHAPTER 10: Incentive. 45
CHAPTER 11: Fun. 47

Pillar III: Mental Toughness: "Do you have the mental skills needed to handle the adversity along the way?" 53

CHAPTER 12: Mental Toughness Is a Choice. 55
CHAPTER 13: Embrace the Pressure. 57
CHAPTER 14: Practice for the Emergencies. 61
CHAPTER 15: Paint a Masterpiece. 67
CHAPTER 16: Trust Your Talent 73
CHAPTER 17: Persevere. 81

Pillar IV: Noble Heart: "Will the lives of others be enhanced in a significant way when you reach your goal?" 86

CHAPTER 18: Selfless Exceptionalism. 89
CHAPTER 19: Choosing a Noble Heart 91
CHAPTER 20: Your Personal Greatness Letter 99
CHAPTER 21: The Final Frontier. 101

Final Thoughts. 109
About the Author 111

References

"I'm a big fan of David Cook. He is one of the most outstanding mental coaches anywhere. I highly recommend greatness. *You'll get so much out of it. It will improve the quality of your life and the people whose lives you touch."*

Ken Blanchard
Chief spiritual officer, The Ken Blanchard Companies
Co-author, *The New One Minute Manager®* and
Servant Leadership in Action

"Dr. Cook prepared me for the battlefield of life. Whether playing competitive golf or flying my F-16 over Iraq, his techniques have always helped me perform at the highest levels. The greatness *book is the culmination of his work and a powerful force multiplier for those rare individuals who truly want to be their best."*

Major Dan Rooney
Founder, Folds of Honor; F-16 pilot, PGA Professional

"The principles in greatness *will not only change your life, they will impact others around you. I don't think any of us can comprehend the rewards we will reap from having a mindset of greatness."*

Lucas Black
Actor, *Seven Days in Utopia, Friday Night Lights, Sling Blade, All the Pretty Horses, Tokyo Drift, Get Low, NCIS New Orleans*

"In your hands is a Picasso. In these few pages, Dr. David Cook has provided you an action plan to create your own masterpiece to greatness. Greatness is your choice! This book will help you learn how to choose to perform your best when it counts the most. Enjoy and apply greatness."

David Cottrell
Author, *Monday Morning Leadership*

"David has built a roadmap for greatness that is anchored by clear goals and a servant leader perspective. David continues to demonstrate his expertise in unlocking the full potential in all of us and making sure we are all ready to perform when it counts most."

Sam Reese
Chief Executive Officer, Vistage Worldwide

"David Cook has devoted his life to the study of performing your best on game day. As a player, coach, and business consultant, he has experienced and helped others find greatness. Whether your game day is on the course or in the boardroom, his practical approach provides a roadmap to elevate your game."

Barry E. Davis
Executive Chairman, EnLink Midstream

References

"One of my greatest desires as a coach is for my players to make their teammates better on and off the court. I also want to see them rise to the occasion when it means the most—game day. David has given us a road map for both in greatness."

Scott Drew
Baylor Men's Basketball Coach

"David has written a great book that gets right to the big issues. What does it take to be successful and what separates the successful from the really great? I loved the stories that illustrate his timeless truths. This book gives us the tools to be better at whatever we do. It shows how to use those successes to invest in others and achieve greatness. I will read this simple but profound book often as I do my best to achieve success and greatness in my own life. I know you will be inspired to greatness too! Enjoy the journey!!"

Scott Simpson
1987 US Open Champion (PGA Tour)

"Dr. David Cook combines his extraordinary life experiences with his gifts of kindness, passion, and faith to deliver wisdom and insights to each of us through his greatness book. My life and the lives of my colleagues have been significantly enhanced because of Dr. Cook's engagement with us."

Randy Eisenman
Co-founder and Managing Partner, Satori Capital

Acknowledgments

The SFT Fraternity, a group of adventurers who provide the encouragement, camaraderie, and financial support for this and other books, made the publishing of this book possible. Thank you to Carson McDaniel, John Vann, Rick Gasser, Jeff Reynolds, Tom Landry, David Jones, Steve Kerns, Bert Lohse, Randy Price, Tom Koos, Buzz Baker, Randy Kenworthy, and George Hanlon. I love the many golf and fishing adventures that we have shared along the way.

Foreword

I'm a big fan of David Cook. When he asked me to write the foreword for his book *greatness*, I was excited because I think he is one of the most outstanding mental coaches anywhere.

I first met David when he came to speak at an annual golf retreat at the incomparable Pine Valley Golf Club I had attended for several years. As anyone who has ever played golf knows, it's really more of a mental game than a physical one. I've never forgotten the pre-shot routine David taught us that weekend: *see*, *feel*, and *trust*. This book goes well beyond that simple approach.

In *greatness*, David describes greatness as *selfless exceptionalism*. That resonates with me in three ways.

First is the difference between success and significance. Too many leaders focus only on success. They think their success depends on how much wealth they accumulate, how much recognition they get, and their power and status. There is nothing wrong with any of those descriptors of success as long as they don't define who you are—because if this is the way you measure your self-worth, the only way you can maintain it is to get *more* money, recognition, and power and status. But when you move from success to significance you focus on the opposite of each of those things. The opposite of accumulation of wealth is generosity of your time, talent, and treasure. The opposite of recognition is service to others. And the opposite of power and status is loving relationships. When you focus on significance—which is similar in many ways to David Cook's description of selfless exceptionalism—you'll be amazed at how much success will come your way. For example, Mother Teresa couldn't have cared less about money, recognition, or power and status. She was all about generosity, service, and loving relationships. And yet, people were falling all over her to give her money, recognition, and power and status. To me, selfless exceptionalism will generate the same return on investment.

The second way that David's work resonates with me is in my passion for servant leadership. In a recent book I co-edited with Renee Broadwell entitled *Servant Leadership in Action*, which includes essays from 44 practitioners and thought leaders in the field, we emphasize that serving others as a leader is an inside-out job. It's all about your character and intentions. Are you here to serve or be served? When you lead with a serving heart—which David calls a *noble heart*—you create, in his words, "high achieving individuals who make those around them and the world better."

Finally, David takes goal setting to a whole new level. There is no doubt that all good performance starts with clear goals—and David will show you how to set goals and accomplish them in a very useful and creative way. He goes beyond *One Minute Goal* setting, and it's worth the extra effort!

Foreword

This is a long-winded way of saying I really like this book and I recommend it highly. You'll get so much out of it. It will improve the quality of your life and the people whose lives you touch.

Ken Blanchard
Chief spiritual officer, The Ken Blanchard Companies
Co-author: *The New One Minute Manager*® and
Servant Leadership in Action

Introduction

It is not uncommon for us to invest $100 on a nice meal, tickets to a sporting event, or a play or concert, a nice bottle of wine, or green fees at a decent course only to have those experiences dissipate like a morning fog. My dear friend and mentor, the late Zig Ziglar, told me that the two things that will change us in the next five years will be the people we meet and the books we read.

Either you or someone who believes in you invested $100 on this collector's edition book. I wrote this book for those willing to invest in their future or the future of someone they care about deeply. However it happened, it is a true privilege to have you join me on this journey.

I contemplated deeply, prayed fervently, and counseled many before choosing this method of distribution. You are about to join me on an intimate journey. I have spent nearly four decades in locker rooms, behind the bench, inside the ropes, or in the boardroom observing and teaching these principles. They are a treasure to me and soon to be for you. This is the culmination of my life's work. It has been a priceless view to "greatness," a vantage point few if any have ever experienced. While the price of the book may limit the number of readers, the impact on those who made the investment will be priceless. In the words of Zig, my prayer is that this is one of those books that changes your life and the lives of those around you.

Speaking about this topic to hundreds of organizations and teams and coaching thousands of elite performers in business, sport, and life has been my mission in my adult life. But to put these principles down on paper was another story. I knew there was more, and I didn't want to jump the gun before I had the complete message to share in book form.

I started the idea for this book with a different title: *The Mindset of a Champion*. But something continued to nag at me. "There is more," I kept hearing. Finally I understood. I waited, and I'm glad for that. Many books have been written about success and champions, but what about that space beyond success, the place of greatness? Greatness is a special trait open to all but earned by few.

I define greatness as "**selfless exceptionalism**." This is the space beyond success. Both of these components are critical to greatness. Without the *selfless* component champions are often egotistical, proud, selfish individuals who serve little beyond their own appetites and interests, becoming poor role models to future champions. They often live lives that are unfulfilled no matter the number, size, or scope of their accomplishments. And without the *exceptionalism* component individuals can sink into mediocrity, eschewing competition and achievement as divisive behaviors that create separation or division between people.

When put together, selfless exceptionalism creates high achieving performers in business, sport, and life whose specific aim is to make those around them and the world better. Their achievements inspire others to greatness, lifting teams, cities, nations, causes, and humanity to new heights. The message of greatness is imperative in our world of adversity, uncertainty, and chaos.

Greatness is reserved for those with a servant's heart and humility. Thus, the small *g* in the book's small title. I've noticed that most book titles seem to scream for attention. Not this one. Its simplicity and size speak to the message inside.

Greatness is expressed most authentically and powerfully as selfless exceptionalism during the defining moments of both life's greatest performance achievements and life's greatest challenges that include uncertainties, adversities, unrest, disasters, setbacks, defeats, chaos, political upheaval, and social disunity among other things. Selfless exceptionalism during the tough times becomes the foundation of thriving versus surviving.

You have to win the inner game in both the mind and heart to reach greatness. There is fierce opposition to both in the competitive arenas of life. The interference on game day in business, sport, and life is chaotic, easily distracting the mind's focus. And the heart—well let's just say that the pull of the world to steal your higher purpose and joy can be stifling.

This book is your road map to greatness. May it inspire you to dream of your true destiny that lies beyond success or failure. It is filled with the most powerful principles and stories accumulated from my career in sport and performance psychology.

While most of my illustrations are from the sport arena, this is not a sport book. You do not need to like sport to receive these life lessons. I use these illustrations because of their power to create word pictures that will stay with you through life's battles. I also use them because they are authentic to my personal experiences. I watched them unfold up close and personal. Your job is to ask yourself how to creatively apply the principle specifically to your performance or leadership arena.

This is a book about performance and leadership principles that can be applied to any aspect of life. For nearly four decades I have shared these ideas and stories with high achievers in some of the most respected organizations in the world including Insperity, Exxon Mobil, Sprint, HP/Compaq, USAA, Vistage International, Heinz, Raytheon, Frito Lay, Whole Foods, Valero, Memorial Hermann Hospitals of Houston, Ameriprise, Merrill Lynch, Bristol-Myers Squibb, Texas Instruments, Bayer, Interstate Battery, Conoco/Phillips, and more. In each case they saw beyond the context of the stories and adapted the principles into their ascent to success. And so shall you.

CHAPTER 1

THE GREATEST PREDICTOR OF SUCCESS

Focus. Passion. Mental toughness. That's it. When these three elements are combined, they become the greatest predictor of success, or exceptionalism, as we will refer to it in this book. These elements also serve as the first three pillars to greatness. The fourth pillar, the one related to the selfless variable of greatness, will be introduced later in the book. In other words:

1. *Where do you want to go? (Focus)*
2. *How bad do you want to get there? (Passion)*
3. *Do you have the mental skills needed to handle the adversity along the journey? (Mental toughness)*

The depth and clarity with which you answer these questions says it all. I have never met a competitor in business, sport, or life who desires to fail. However, I meet daily with performers who consistently fail to reach their true potential when it means the most—game day. They don't fail because they don't try; they fail because of their answers to these three questions. They fail because they are missing a few pieces to the performance puzzle. It isn't because they are weak in character; it's not because of poor strategy, training, or technique; it isn't because they lack strength or fitness. They just lack knowledge about the mental game.

Unlocking the potential that has been endowed to you as a human and that you further have earned through sacrifice, hard work, and practice is the purpose for this book. I want you to realize your dreams on game day.

We all get it. It's easy to perform well when not on the stage. It is something very different to "perform your best when it means the most." I'll teach you the secrets of rising to the occasion during those defining moments in your life. You were created to be exceptional. Especially during the tough times.

The journey through the forest of naysayers, the gravitational force of mediocrity, and the seductive call from the false sirens hold you back from greatness. It's inside of you to be exceptional. Whether you are in business, sport, or performing in life, the information is the same. It will take a commitment to focus, passion, and mental toughness.

It is in the intricacies of achieving each of these initial three pillars along with the fourth that I will introduce later that you will find the treasure you seek. Let's start with a story of one of the greatest athletes I have worked with. Everyone around him assumed he had a bullet proof mental game.

I got a call from the assistant GM of the San Antonio Spurs late one night asking that I catch a flight the next day to the site of an NBA game on the West Coast. I served as the team mental training coach for the Spurs for eight seasons that included two NBA championships. This story took place in the middle of that time.

The Spurs were quickly falling behind the other teams in their division that particular year. It was uncharacteristic for them, as they were the previous year's NBA champions. At the time of the call, they were nearing the halfway point of the regular season. Their superstar Tim Duncan was mired in a slump. Most noticeably his free throw shooting had dropped from around 75 percent for his career to 47 percent for the year. The other teams were on to this. They were intentionally fouling him to make it worse and to shine an unwanted spotlight on this situation. The Spurs were now fourth in the division they were accustomed to dominating. They were heading in the wrong direction. The management knew this was a critical situation, potentially career threatening for Tim.

To this day Tim remains one of the most exceptional athletes with whom I have worked. He is a man of character, highly motivated, focused, and passionate about competing and winning. He was mentally tough and willing to do anything his coaches asked of him. He was and is a true champion. His coaches were the best in the business. Tim was simply experiencing a major slump and the team record reflected it.

When I arrived at the team hotel, the coach Gregg Popovich put Tim and me in a room and made it clear this wasn't a mechanical issue, but something that had gotten in Tim's head. "Doc is the head doctor so you guys work this out." And with that he left us to go to work.

It would have been easy for Tim to balk at this but he was all in. He put his mind and heart into the process I taught—incorporating a new **focus**, investing in the process with **passion**, and responding to the challenge with new elements of **mental toughness**. Coach Popovich, a Hall of Fame, no-nonsense, old school coach, who doesn't put up with pop psychobabble, unselfishly opened the door to our work. He trusted me and the information I brought to the table. To his credit, Pop is a lifetime learner and he's open as a leader to providing all the tools needed to support the play of his players and coaches.

Here's what happened. I met with Tim on a Wednesday. We talked late into the evening creating a plan and then applied it on the court during the shoot around the following morning. While others looked on, Tim blocked out the distractions and meticulously applied the principles that I will share in this book. The Spurs played the leading team in the division on a very hostile court that evening after our initial work. Tim had 36 points, 21 rebounds, and made 6 of 9 (66 percent) from the free throw line in the game of his life. He had a similar game two days later on the NBC game of the week where he scored over 30 points against another leading team, then finished the road trip with a stellar performance two days later in California. On Tuesday of the following week (less than a week from our initial meeting), the man mired in the deepest slump of his career was named NBA player of the week for his stellar performances in those three road games. He shattered the slump.

I asked him to commit to the new mental process for 10 games and then at the end we would analyze outcome numbers, but not until then. In the first 10 games he went from 47 percent to 62 percent from the line. His entire game turned around as well. He committed to doing the same for 10 more games. He averaged 75 percent from the free throw line in those next 10 games. The best stat of all … one year later Tim earned MVP of the league and shot 80 percent from the line for the year.

Tim's success story can be your story, too, by overcoming interference and adversity and pressing through to a breakthrough. When we met, Tim *had* talent; he simply didn't have these principles. It's time to open a new chapter to your career in business, sport, or life armed with the greatness principles.

PILLAR I:
FOCUS

"Where do you want to go?"

CHAPTER 2

Twenty Minutes Before the Trophy Celebration

The first step on this journey to greatness is to identify where you want to go. Take a moment and picture metaphorically the trophy you would like to hold one day—the job title, the position, accomplishment, ownership of a business or home, tournament victory, a championship, MVP, a stage performance, acting role, earning potential, degree, Academy Award, authoring a book, maybe even a best seller. The options are boundless. And just to be clear, we often have several goals at the same time. The process is the same for each of them.

This vision establishes a compass heading and provides an initial focus. It is the true north of your heart and desire. It is the critical first step on the journey. But it is only the penultimate step in the process.

The most critical step is next. Create an image of what it looks like 20 minutes before the trophy celebration. That is a very different yet real picture. To eventually hold a trophy we all have to go through the 20 minutes before the trophy celebration. It is a place of intense pressure. Mental chaos is raining down and the internal and external interference is stifling. For you this may literally be 20 minutes before the trophy celebration, or it becomes a metaphor for the defining moments or breakthroughs on your journey. Either way you need to exit the comfort zone now. This is anything but comfortable.

I have heard far too often from performers following a misstep during these defining moments. They describe the scene, wishing that they had made different mental choices. They realize too late that they were taken out of their game by the chaos. They simply come to the conclusion they weren't mentally prepared. It generally has very little to do with talent and everything to do with lack of awareness of the mindset that must be implemented to win in that environment.

Every word in this book is to prepare you for these championship-defining moments. These moments don't come along every day but be prepared as if they do. And often, they come during the tough times of life.

Let's start with the first pillar: Focus. Let me ask you a simple question: "Can you give more than 100 percent?"

In high school I had a football coach who used to bark out things like, "You better give 110 percent today or you'll lose. If you don't give 110 percent, you'll be on the bench before you know it!" He was also our math teacher. In the classroom 100 percent was defined as a universe, complete, full, no room for more. But in football practice, he wanted and demanded more. I never pointed out the discrepancy. His nickname was "Pit Bull."

Isn't that the goal? Leaving it all in the arena? Giving 100 percent? Maybe that should be our focus. However, I've discovered that there is a better focus than to "try to give 100 percent."

Back in graduate school I had a chance to scientifically answer this question. I was required to develop and deliver a single subject experimental design research project that would answer a significant question while at the same time enabling me to conjecture the findings to the population as a whole. Everything had to be set up with precision, and I needed the perfect subject. To answer the question "can you give more than 100 percent" I needed a subject who wouldn't quit. I needed a tough minded and motivated competitor. I found one: a marine who had run 21 marathons. He was trained to take a bullet and to push himself to his physical limit over and over.

He agreed to a series of physical stamina tests. The same test would be given across a five-week period—one test per week. The test consisted of walking on a treadmill until it was physically impossible for him to take another step. The catch was that I would increase the incline, systematically creating difficulty and intensity that would lead to agonizing pain the longer he walked. He agreed to this because he was challenged to finish at the top of the established index of years of research. He wanted to "win" the event. I had to let him know this wasn't a competition as much as it was a measure of fitness level so that an accurate training regimen could be prescribed for those who took the test. Nevertheless, he was motivated to finish in the top percentile of the thousands who had taken this test across the country for years.

I hooked him up to the heart monitor, faced the treadmill toward a cinder block wall, removed all timing devices from the room, and gave him one command: "Give me 100 percent; don't stop until you can't stand up."

That was fuel to this marine. He lived for those words. His performance was amazing; he didn't break a sweat until around the 20-minute mark. At 26 minutes he was in complete agony. Sweat was flying, spit was flying, his heart was about to blow out of his chest. He clawed his way to 27 minutes, gasping for air before crashing to his knees as I hit the stop button.

I helped him off the treadmill to a chair where he recovered. Catching his breath, he asked how he had done. His words were "Did I win?" At this point I lied. For the sake of my research, I told him he was amazing and had gone much further than most and was in the top one percent of all those who had taken part in this particular stress test regimen. I told him he had gone 28 minutes instead of his actual 27. He was pleased.

Before he left, I asked if he thought he could take one more step the following week. I asked if he believed he could go 28.01. He said it would be hard but he would recover, train, and come back ready to beat his time. I wrote 28 minutes on a piece of paper and told him to tape it to his mirror and surround himself with the number 28 for the week. I let him know that he would have a clock to monitor his progress when he returned for round two.

He returned with extra incentive the following week. He was pleased to find an old-fashioned three-foot diameter timer clock placed directly in front of the treadmill. I kept everything else the same as it had been the week before. However, just before we started the treadmill, I gave him a different command. "Beat 28."

His heart rate responded identically to the previous test. Nearing the 27-minute mark, he was in extreme pain. But he kept his attention on the clock and was able to go 28 minutes and 10 seconds. He went 70 seconds further than the previous test—in absolute agony! I was impressed.

I sent him away after this session with no number to focus on and just said I would see him the following week. He hurt so badly that he was just glad to leave.

He returned the following week excited to break his previous record. Just before the test I reverted to the command from the first week: "Give me 100 percent; don't stop until you can't stand up." He responded, "Where is the clock?" I answered that I thought he could break the record again if he would give 100 percent. He walked 26 minutes and thought he had set the world record. And, I told him he had gone 28 minutes and 15 seconds. He was pleased. I wrote that number on a piece of paper so that he could focus on it again all week, and I let him know he would have the clock the following week.

He had a bounce in his step as he arrived the next week knowing he would have the clock. With the clock he again went beyond the goal. For the final week of testing, I once again took the clock away. No clock, no way—he finished at 26 minutes and 30 seconds.

When I told him the truth at the end of the study, he could not believe the discrepancy. We both learned a great lesson, one that literally could be conjectured to others. The truth is you can give more than 100 percent. Not in actual reality of physical limits, but in the sense that we all have a reservoir of potential left in the tank at the end of the game, day, performance, deal, or whatever the end point is. The key is tapping into the reservoir so that we come closer to reaching our potential when it means the most.

So what is the secret to focus? When dissecting the experiment, four foundational principles of goal orientation emerge. First and foremost we know that those who set goals outperform those who don't. Research is clear on that. The most robust of all findings in the performance psychology literature revolve around this truth. But let's take it a step further. Let's take the goal setting group, the high performers, and let's split them into high achievers and champions. Why do some in the high-performance group outperform others? What does it take to become the best of the best? That is the question that has motivated me throughout my career and should light a fire within your curiosity.

    This is the secret. I have never seen this in a book. Those who become champions set different types of goals than others. Their goals have four distinct elements: they are specific, tangible, difficult, and self-referenced. That is the secret.

CHAPTER 3

SPECIFIC GOALS

Specific goals move you further than subjective or "do my best" goals. When there is a well thought out, specific, measurable goal, you will accomplish more. It creates specificity of focus.

In our experiment for giving more than 100 percent, it was clear that a number on the clock was better fuel, even for a marine, than simply trying to give his best. When he had a measurable goal, he was able to know where he stood at all times. This allowed him to narrow his focus and block out the pain or interference that was loudest in his head. When you are attempting to break through a barrier, your intensity of focus is critical.

The professional and elite golfers that I coach are challenged to turn in two scores after a tournament round. The first is their actual outcome score. The second is their concentration (or focus) score. Without this second score there is no specificity in measuring the inner game. It would be too easy for them to say, "I tried to give 100 percent today," or "My inner game was pretty good," or "I didn't think well today." All of those are non-specific. To win the inner game you have to go further than a subjective measure.

With my golfers I developed a 15-second pre-shot focus process based on three words: see, feel, and trust. If they accomplish the process on the shot, they get a check. They keep track on each shot during the competition. They get a check if they go through the process before each shot; no check if something steals their concentration and they fail to incorporate the process. This becomes their number one goal for the day: to put their mind in position to succeed. It is the one thing they have 100 percent control of. We define this by the see, feel, trust process. It gives them control. This is the same process Tim Duncan embraced when overcoming his free throw slump. See, feel, trust defines the neural pathway to success.

In the end they have an outcome score which might be level par at 72. Their focus score is generally less for first timers, around 60 or so. Dividing 60 by 72 gives us their grade for the day, a specific measurement as to the percentage of time they accomplished their focus goal. In this case it would be 83 percent or a B-. I give them the goal of getting to 85 percent at first and then move it up as they progress. It becomes a very specific, measurable way to quantify their success in winning the inner game and moves it out of the subjective category.

Furthermore, this hole-by-hole specific grading allows me to see on which holes they failed to reach their goal. We then have a specific conversation around the situation on that hole, giving us insight into the focus stealing elements that caused the glitch. It is at that point we can prepare specific strategies for attacking these elements in the future. Specific measurable goals are essential for winning the mental game. I have used this process creatively in business settings and across all sports.

    Begin to develop a new and focused goal. Create it so that it can be specifically defined. It may change drastically by the end of this book, so hold on to it loosely until the end. Have fun with this process, chapter by chapter.

CHAPTER 4

TANGIBLE GOALS

Putting a goal or a symbol of the goal in a tangible place where you can see it creates depth to your focus.

By strategically placing his goal in prominent places, our marine made his goal tangible. He could see it and touch it. It was imprinting in his mind throughout the run up to game day, thus deepening his focus. It inspired and motivated him daily. Making your goal tangible is the antidote to the loud call of mediocrity and the caving in to the limiting thoughts that distract you from becoming great.

Besides asking PGA Tour players to keep track of their concentration score, I also ask them to make it tangible. They are encouraged to mark their golf ball with the first letters of their three-word process: SFT (see, feel, trust). That way, no matter where they find their ball or what kind of mental challenges they may face, their focus goal is staring back at them from the ground. It is a tangible reminder during the good and the bad of the round to stay committed to their focus process.

I was well into my thirties when competing in the Kansas Amateur golf tournament one year in Lawrence, Kansas. I was the director of Applied Sport Psychology at the University of Kansas at the time, and I had made it into the match play portion of the event. As I approached the rules official on the first tee to declare my ball, I said, "I'm playing a Titleist 2 with three letters, SFT, written on it." To the surprise of the official, my college-age competitor chimed in, "I'm playing a Titleist 3 with SFT marked on it." The other player looked at me and said with a smile, "I've been to your seminar."

While sitting in the stands of a collegiate baseball game a few years back with a former player and current booster of the highly ranked team, he asked me to watch their All-American pitcher before each pitch. I watched carefully as he took one final look at his glove before he started his pitching move. The booster told me the pitcher had written SFT on his glove as a reminder to go through the see, feel, trust process before each pitch. Unbeknownst to me this pitcher had read my first book, *Seven Days in Utopia*, where SFT was first proposed. He took it to heart.

In a recent season with another NBA team, I was coaching a player who had just signed a major deal with the team. It was a dream contract. The problem for him and for many of us is that this kind of deal can become a distraction. Success can breed fear. Success will always come with new interference points. Thoughts come that can take you out of your game—thoughts like "now I have to live up to this new expectation," or "now I have to be perfect all the time to be deserving of this," or "what if I fail in front of all these people who know about my new contract," or "I have to be Superman now." The key to winning the inner game when the thought storms rage is to be able to fight off the onslaught with your tangible goal close to mind. We win when our focus is riveted on our specific goal. It is our foundation.

This NBA player found his true north by writing SFT on the toes of each of his game day shoes. Whenever the battle in his mind would flare up, he simply looked down and locked in to his goal. His goal was to stay in his process: See, Feel, Trust. He was able to stay focused and steadfast during the intense 82-game season and help his team receive a playoff berth. His attitude turned from fear to passion. He loved playing again, and his joy for the game returned. It affected everyone around him but most of all it affected his play. He found his rhythm once again.

For cross-country teams I advocate that during their practice runs they choose three to five tangible objects at strategic points along the course. These tangible objects then become mental signposts that contain their strategy for that portion of the course. It can be a hill, stream, rock outcropping, tree, flat area, etc. The evening before the race they write their overall race strategy incorporating these tangible objects. They carry this paper to the event and read it just before the race. These objects become tangible self-coaching markers along the way that help guide their focus and strategy.

Create a tangible way to have your goal displayed where you have to interact with it several times each day.

CHAPTER 5

DIFFICULT GOALS

Goal setting is an art—easy goals demotivate; impossible goals exasperate. A difficult goal pushes you beyond the norm. It causes a determined focus.

Setting goals is truly an art. It takes creativity to get them just right. And often you have to be willing to adjust them because of unforeseen situations (injuries, accidental environmental or personal happenings, changes of direction, etc.). I had a deep desire and goal to become a professional golfer early in life. I wanted to play in the US Open one day. Along the way during my collegiate golf career that door was closing as the sport psychology door was opening. I had given my all to becoming a pro. It was hard to switch gears, but the lessons I learned from the original difficult goal transferred to the new difficult goal of pursuing a Ph.D. in Applied Sport Psychology.

Fast-forward several years. I can remember the day I was attending the US Open at Oakmont Country Club. The conditions were brutal. I was working with two players competing in the US Open at the time. At one point it hit me. I was outside the ropes on game day making a significant contribution to the two players inside the ropes. They were playing great in the toughest conditions I had ever seen. I was thankful to be at the US Open on the outside of the ropes rather than on the inside. I would have shot a 90 if I were on the other side of the ropes, not knowing then what I know now. My initial goal had changed, but I had accomplished my new difficult goal of becoming a sport psychology professional. I was thankful for exactly where I was and what I was doing at the US Open—it was poignant. Difficult goals will lead to the treasure you are seeking, or they will become the catalyst and experience needed for your next goal adventure.

    Our marine gave it his all that first week. We set a difficult goal for his second week but one that he thought was doable (he thought it was one step further). He wanted to get better. It was in his marine DNA to continue to improve, and this difficult goal became his focus. He shattered his goal by reaching deeper and going further than he had previously. Unbeknownst to him, I had set a more aggressive goal for him with the extra minute I added. In the end, the more difficult goal I had chosen for him inspired him to exceed his expectations.

    Continuing with the golf example from chapter three, my first goal for a player is to strive for a solid B, 85 percent, for their concentration score. This is a difficult but attainable specific goal. Through my playing experience I understand how difficult it is to compete for four hours with intense interference all the while maintaining focus. While difficult, it is possible, and if they come close to it, invariably their scores reflect their accomplishment. Eventually I challenge them to be in the 90 percent range each time. Few have made it to 100 percent.

   One memorable week, I was coaching a mini tour player who received a sponsor's exemption into a PGA Tour event. His name is Stan Utley. He took my difficult challenge to score above 85 percent. His concentration score for the four days was solidly in the 90 percent range. He did this in the face of huge interference and mental chaos as a mini tour player paired against some of the best players in the world. He made an A on the inner game, and he took home the trophy! He won against many of the best players in the world, and by doing so he earned a two-year exemption on the PGA Tour and reached one of his lifetime goals—to be a winner on the PGA Tour. Stan eventually became one of the most accomplished short game instructors in the profession. He often shares this story with his students and incorporates this difficult goal in their games as well.

   As you continue to read, in the back of your mind begin to identify a difficult goal that is neither too easy nor impossible. Save it until the end, because there is a chance your vision and desire may change in the final few chapters.

CHAPTER 6
SELF-REFERENCED GOALS

A self-referenced goal is a goal measured against self. In the goal setting process, the truest measure of success is you against you yesterday. It causes an inspired focus.

In almost everything you do, someone is always better and someone worse. Comparison against others may be inevitable in competition, but it isn't the best reference point in the goal setting process.

I remember a TV interview with Tiger Woods many years ago when he was in his prime, winning many times each year. He had noticeably changed his swing for the first time. The interviewer asked him why he changed his swing when he was already the best in the world. I was impressed with his completely self-referenced response. He simply said, "One, two, one." The interviewer probed for the meaning. Tiger said, "Since improving my swing that is my finish in the last three majors: first, second, and first." Tiger didn't compare himself to everyone else and rest on his talent; he wanted to better his own major record. He wanted the grand slam.

Chasing someone else's record can be inspiring, but what really gets you there is to improve against yourself yesterday. Once you catch up to them you keep right on going because your goal is not done. Your true goal is to continue to become better than yesterday. And let me be very clear here. Changing technique is not always the way to get better as Tiger eventually learned after several more attempts at swing changes. Mastering the inner game by applying the principles from this book and learning and implementing something from each performance experience are major ways to improve against self. And sometimes, maintaining your current pace and style of play with patience is the way to break personal records as well. In fact, "patience" is a very good and difficult goal for most of us.

Recent research shows us that the human brain isn't wired for perfection. It's wired to adapt. This is ground breaking information. It may literally change the way we prepare for all performances in life. I emphasize in my golf training to focus on becoming the best adapter rather than the best swinger. We can always improve against ourselves in adapting, learning new shots, or by getting better from difficult lies or situations. Most people hit a wall in technical training at some point and can become discouraged. Learning to play the game with more shots in the bag, in my opinion, opens the door wider for improvement on game day. The brain has unlimited capacity in the adapting category, but it is limited in the perfection category.

Describe your goal in terms of its being self-referenced. What do you have to do today to be better tomorrow and so on?

In summary, the secret to a bulletproof focus is to strategically set specific, tangible, difficult, and self-referenced goals. All things being equal in terms of talent, these four strategies are the first steps that separate champions from others when applied to both the inner game and the external game.

PILLAR II:
PASSION

"How bad do you want to get there?"

CHAPTER 7

The Fuel of Passion

The second separation factor between good performers and greatness is passion. Great performers have a desire, determination, or motivation that is almost otherworldly. We call this passion. It is a sold-out compulsion to reach a dream or goal. A lot of us would like to climb a tall mountain, but few of us actually do it.

Having specific, tangible, difficult, self-referenced goals is not the end of the journey. There is more. Those goals must have rocket fuel in the form of passion added to them. What fuels passion?

When I was a professor and the sport psychologist at the University of Kansas, one of my favorite coaches, Rick Attig, was the jumps coach in track and field. Rick started every season by having his pole-vaulters establish their personal goals for the season. He kept a copy of them in his desk just in case he had an issue with lack of passion from any of his athletes.

One elite vaulter showed up with high goals and aspirations. He started well but then discovered the freedoms of college in general and sororities in particular. He started coming to practice with less enthusiasm and looking a little unkempt. His training was suffering. Coach called him into the office and pulled his goal sheet out and set it on the desk between them. He then pulled out a red marker and scratched through each goal and lowered them all. This got the attention of the young vaulter, who objected. The coach replied, "My job besides coaching my athletes is to protect them. I'm protecting you from great disappointment. You don't have the passion needed to reach the goals you set, so I lowered them to a level you can reach with your current attitude. However, the adjusted goals are not good enough to make the team. I'll give you a week, and if your passion has improved, we'll adjust your goals and determine at that point if they're high enough to make the team."

Because of the accountability process, the athlete saw the problem and changed his attitude and passion. He decided to mature. The following week the coach said he had seen a change but only enough to adjust the goals slightly. He said he needed to see more. The coach continued this for several weeks until his young budding superstar was transformed into a passionate and focused athlete on a mission. In the end he accomplished his goals for the season, and the coach succeeded in using this accountability process to protect him from failure.

CHAPTER 8

OWNERSHIP

The first element that fuels passion is ownership of the goal. We know that when there is an absolute buy-in to the goal, passion is increased. If someone else sets the goal or if you set the goal to please someone else, it is less motivating than if you create it and own it.

Generally speaking, your passion is greater for those things you own than for someone else's stuff. Why? Investment. You own it. Ownership brings a heightened awareness of its value and cost, and taking care of your investment motivates you.

In the same way, those goals you craft and into which you put thought along with inspiration will create a deeper fire than someone else forcing their goals or agenda upon you. Wise leaders tap into this power by setting up a process that promotes individual ownership.

The first year I arrived at KU as a 27-year-old rookie sport psychologist, my first call was from our Hall of Fame basketball coach, Larry Brown. I had patiently worked through all the schooling and studying and internships and degrees to get to this point. It was now time to test my mettle. This would be an ultimate test for me right off the bat.

Coach Brown said he had an issue that he hoped I could help with. He had a very selfish team, especially his highly touted freshman class, and he needed a plan to create team cohesion. I told him I'd be glad to help. To my surprise he said he'd be right over to my office.

As he described the situation, I began to notice each player blamed the others for the rampant selfishness that existed throughout the team. I had an idea based on the principle of ownership. I suggested that I meet with each player individually and ask him what he would do to create team unity. By doing this I would get his investment into the solution. I believed each of them would come up with similar ideas, and in the end the plan we would install would have each player's ownership embedded within it.

Coach Brown had them all come to my office the next day, one by one. As I thought, each of them basically said they really wanted team unity, and they thought it was important. They also blamed the others. When they told me their ideas to help eliminate the selfishness, I asked if they were committed to doing what they said. They all agreed.

The following day I had accumulated a list of 10 "commandments" of team unity for this team that they had basically established. They liked them because the commandments were their words, ideas, and actions. At the bottom of the page, we had a commitment statement with a place for each of their signatures. Coach cautioned them not to sign it unless they were willing to do it. They all signed, and we made copies and placed them on the doors of their lockers so that they were visible each day. Coach now had a plan/goal for team unity that the team owned. He knew that he now had the power to hold them accountable. I believe if he had come up with his own list and forced it on them, they would have balked. Instead, they got over themselves, committed to that piece of paper, and this freshman class won the NCAA national championship when they were seniors.

This principle worked in my life as well. My dad was an engineer. He always put food on the table and had a stable job. He really thought it was a good plan and best that his boys become good engineers as well. His goal for my life, while noble, just didn't inspire the dreams rising inside of me. I slogged through school as an average student in engineering until my sophomore year of college when I changed my major to pursue something else. I didn't know what it was going to be, but I just knew engineering was not something I owned. My dad worked through it with me and said that whatever I did, I needed to do it with my whole heart. That was very different than pursuing something he wanted with his whole heart for me. I obviously appreciated having a dad who cared about me, but my heart moved in a different direction.

When I discovered sport psychology, I found my passion. I owned it. I pursued a Ph.D., my grades skyrocketed, and my interest ignited. I owned my goal, and it changed my life.

I see it all the time in sport: kids trying to live up to a parent's goal for them. The parent, wondering why the child isn't motivated, sends them to me. Until the child determines to set their own goal and own it, they will live in one of two worlds. On one side of the equation, they will lack the passion needed to get there. Their interest will waver because they lack full buy-in to their parent's goal. Or, on the other side of the equation, they will live in constant fear of letting down their parent who set the goal. The pressure and guilt to live up to a parent's vicarious goal can become suffocating. Either scenario becomes a debilitating factor in long-term success.

The same thing happens in business. A boss or committee sends down the goals for the organization without soliciting input from people on the front lines. There was no member collaboration or input so the impersonal goals have a tendency to create fear rather than inspire passion. When a company runs off the fear of imposed and impersonal goals, the order of the day will be strife, turnover, disunity, and distrust.

What do you need to do to take ownership of your dreams and goals?

CHAPTER 9

ACCOUNTABILITY

We know that goals are most often accomplished when there is accountability to the goal. In other words, shared goals tend to take us further than if we keep them to ourselves. Finding someone who has your best interest at heart and with whom you can share your goals is imperative.

In the story in the last section, Coach Brown created ownership first so that accountability could happen. Once we had the team buy in to shared goals, they owned the 10 commandments of team cohesion for that team at that moment in time. It was at that point that Coach Brown could use them to keep the players' behavior in check. Accountability was the process that kept the goal alive and well for years to come.

Let me demonstrate this on a micro level with another example. I had a PGA Tour player, Steve Lowery, who had lost his way and was just showing up without a goal at each tournament site. Consequently, he was struggling through each round, hoping something good would eventually happen. He was rudderless and had just missed five cuts in a row because of this. He was regressing to overly mechanical thoughts and failing to play the game in front of the ball.

We discussed getting back to being himself and playing the kind of golf he enjoyed—creative golf, shaping shots, playing by feel. So we established a goal together not to hit a shot without "calling his shot" out loud to me. In other words he had to describe his target, the shape of the shot, and the trajectory. These are the three elements to visualizing a golf shot. He liked that plan, and he started playing well again that day in the practice round. At the end of the round, I asked if he would be willing to have his caddie be involved when I was not there on game day. He agreed. We created an accountability plan where his caddie would not hand him a club until he verbally "called his shot" to his caddie.

This plan created a missing passion for the game and opened new communications between them. Steve played great. On the following Sunday, he was in the hunt. On the 17th hole he made a brilliant eagle three on the par five, which propelled him to his first victory on the PGA Tour. Accountability to the goal changed Steve's destiny that day. I'll tell you the rest of his amazing story in a later chapter.

I opened my discussion of passion with the story about the pole-vaulter who had quickly lost his way in college. The coach created a brilliant accountability process that ended up saving this pole-vaulter's career. Even though the coach was tough, he loved this young man and knew the drill. He was in position to use his wisdom to lead. And in so doing he used the accountability process to re-establish the passion for greatness that was still inside his young athlete.

Early in his presidency, John F. Kennedy brilliantly established a passion throughout our country to put a man on the moon by 1969. He established a date and also sparked the imagination of engineers, scientists, mathematicians, pilots, and astronauts for answering this call. The entire country bought into this dream and date. While the Sixties were a tumultuous time, this goal served to keep the country together in a special and unique way. There have been few celebrations so great in my memory than when Neil Armstrong put his foot on the moon in 1969 and declared, "That's one small step for man, one giant leap for mankind."

With whom in your life will you share your goals? Who is it that has your best interests at heart?

CHAPTER 10

Incentive

When a goal leads to a meaningful, tangible prize such as money, a trophy, championship ring, raise, company car, or recognition, it tends to increase passion. Incentives have long been used to sustain passion through the ups and downs of the chase.

I was the mental training coach for the San Antonio Spurs' first and second NBA championship. The incentive to have a ring was a significant motivator for the players during those runs. One of our players, Steve Kerr, already had three rings from other team championships, but he was just as passionate about this one. The ring stood as a symbol that you were a world champion. Only one team could wear that ring each year, and passion ran high for the right to wear it. I was awarded one as well, and I can tell you that it was a major highlight in my professional career. The ring is cool.

Many symbols used in the competitive world signify excellence and success: an Olympic gold medal, a PGA trophy, a gold star in first grade, a merit badge, the dean's list, the Million Dollar Round Table, earning an incentive trip, earning rank in the military, getting a raise in the corporate world, winning a trial, writing a best-seller, recording a number one hit record, earning an Academy Award—all lead to recognition and reward. It is easy to see how you can become so passionate about something with such great ramifications, whether that is a tangible reward or an intangible one.

What internal or external incentive inspires you? Are there incentives you can create for yourself that will propel you to a higher level of passion?

CHAPTER 11

FUN

When the journey toward the goal is encased in fun, passion is sustained.

One of the great experiences that I have had was coaching football at St. Anne's-Belfield in Charlottesville, Virginia, during my doctoral program at the University of Virginia. During the final year of my degree program, I was promoted to head coach. St. Anne's is a small private school that would often wade into the turbulent waters of playing military prep schools. I only had 21 guys on the team, not enough to have offense and defense, so most of them played both ways. My guys were very small but tough. They had won state in lacrosse and mostly played football in the offseason just for fun.

We had two games left in our season. One was against a military school called Miller, located in the Blue Ridge Mountains. Miller was a fine prep school for many aspiring collegiate athletes that needed an extra year to get ready. The final game was a TBA that our AD was working on. He wouldn't divulge the team. As we drove into Miller, we were met by a team of at least 50 players; most of them as I recall were huge guys. To make matters worse, we had to walk into the stadium on their end and pass them as they snickered at our size, number, and plain white uniforms. A cannon was fired after the national anthem that undid our players, as if they weren't intimidated enough already.

On the first play from scrimmage, our best player was hit as he attempted to run up the middle. His jaw was broken and would ultimately be wired shut for the next month. Before he was taken from the field in an ambulance, he fumbled and they recovered. On their first play from scrimmage, our next best player received a career-ending injury and was carried off the field. We were down to 19 players and they were manhandling our guys. We got beat 49-0, and it could have been worse, but they took pity on us.

The following week we had an off week to heal and prepare for our final game. On Monday I gave the team the day off to recover. The AD called me into his office to let me know who our opponent would be for the final game. When he revealed to me that it would be Miller again, I was stunned and thought about refusing to let our team play them for fear of further injury. He was our lacrosse coach and told me that they were tough and wanted another shot. He said I just needed a good game plan. The meeting was over, and I had a choice: quit or find a way.

That evening I did some soul searching and realized that this was an opportunity to test the concept of fun. I could have gone the other direction and used fear as a motivator but chose instead to put into practice what I believed.

Fun

I had grown up playing football in Texas in the Seventies. My specialty as a high school quarterback was the triple option that no one was using at the time, and certainly no one in Virginia high school football. In the triple option the quarterback determines to hand off the ball, keep it, or pitch it, all determined by the movement of the defense as the play is unfolding. Done well, it completely exasperates the defense, especially their defensive tackle, defensive end, and linebacker—in this case their best players. I decided to install it in two weeks' time. The reason: it was novel, it was fun, and it was just what we needed to neutralize the future collegiate stars who were playing defensive end and tackle for Miller.

When our team showed up for practice on Tuesday, I announced our opponent, and that we were going to have fun and run circles around their best players. While they took a big collective gulp, I added that we were going to run two plays for the entire game—option left and option right. I told them we were going to completely let these two guys go (tackle and end), not even try to block them, but instead option off their move and exasperate them. I said that gave us two extra blockers on the other players, including their linebacker, and put us at an advantage. I also said I was going to teach our offensive line how to crab block and tangle up the feet of the other big guys rather than trying to go head-to-head when blocking. I convinced them it would work, it would be fun, and there was no way for Miller to learn how to defend us during the context of the game.

They bought in and we had a glorious 10 days of high-energy fun, backyard-like football practice. I also shared with them that playing the triple option would ground out the clock, and therefore we wouldn't have to be on defense as long.

They loved the new blocking technique that would use physics rather than brute force, and they loved the creative game plan of only having two plays. I told them that whatever side their big defensive end lined up on, that was the side we would option to. We wanted to go right at him and frustrate him. They loved it.

Game day came and our stands were full. We had 19 men on our team suited out. Our guys were great, and the plan worked perfectly. Their superstar defensive end that we optioned off of removed his helmet and threw it to the sidelines at one point in the second quarter as he left the field. He was completely frustrated and humiliated by our ability to simply option off his move. It was perfect!

We were down 6-0 with two minutes to go and were on their three-yard line. If we scored and kicked an extra point, we most likely would have won the game. As often happens when running the option, we fumbled the pitch and lost 6-0. Though we lost, it became the greatest victory in their lives and mine. It was amazing how some "fun" had inspired passion in our rag-tag team and changed their fear to anticipation. I will never forget the unbridled celebration following the game as our opponents watched us in absolute bewilderment. Even though they won on the scoreboard they lost the game.

Can you think of a specific application of fun that you can creatively incorporate into your journey to greatness?

PILLAR III: MENTAL TOUGHNESS

"Do you have the mental skills needed to handle the adversity along the way?"

CHAPTER 12

Mental Toughness Is a Choice

Mental toughness is the ability to reach your potential in the face of adversity, interference, and change. It isn't something you are born with. It comes from observing, mentoring, and learning, as well as from experiencing success and failure along the journey. It isn't part of your DNA. It comes from choices you make in your mind before and during performances. It comes from defining the setting in your favor, putting your mind in position to succeed during performance, and seeing obstacles as challenges rather than setbacks.

It takes volition—the will to choose. At any point in life or in a performance, there are six volitional choices along the volitional scale that we can make: I won't, I can't, I'd like to, I'll try, I can, I will. Mental toughness is established by taking an "I will" to:

- Embracing the pressure
- Practicing for the emergencies
- Painting a masterpiece
- Trusting your talent
- Persevering

CHAPTER 13

EMBRACE THE PRESSURE

Pressure is our greatest competitive ally.

Pressure becomes our greatest competitive ally in the pursuit for greatness. We know the "20 minutes before the trophy celebration" is coming. The only way to be prepared for it is to scrimmage under pressure. Pressure becomes an ally. It gives us a chance to practice volition in the hostile battle for the mind. Mental toughness choices sound good on paper, but they have to be battle tested. Looking for a place to put your foot on the line and feel the heat each day should be a goal. Avoiding pressure leads to failure.

I was working with one of the top pole-vaulters in the world several years back. His name was Scott Huffman. He was preparing for the Olympics that were two years off. His goal was to make the Olympic team. It would be his last event as a professional athlete. He had a specific, tangible, difficult, self-referenced goal that he was passionate about, and it was fueled by ownership, accountability, incentive, and fun. But at breakfast one morning he revealed a crack in the armor.

Scott said he felt so much pressure about his upcoming event, an event that was two years prior to the Olympic Games, and he asked if I could help him not feel the pressure. I asked him where the pressure was coming from. He said the upcoming meet was for the Professional Track and Field Outdoor National Championship, a competition in which he had failed miserably in the past. It was his self-proclaimed nemesis meet. I asked him what his big goal was even though I knew. "The Olympics in two years," he responded. I asked him if there would be any pressure at the Olympics, as a reported four billion people would be viewing it. He said, "Yes."

I then asked him if there would be any pressure at the Olympic trials occurring about eight weeks ahead of the Olympics, setting the stage for him: You have one chance every four years on a track you don't get to choose, against competition you don't get to choose, in weather you don't get to choose, and with a body condition that you can't completely control. You get one shot. And for him it would be his last chance. Again he answered, "Yes." Then I taught him that part of succeeding at the trials and at the Olympics would be jumping with extreme pressure and thriving on it in the meantime. It would literally become his ultimate "20 minutes before the trophy celebration." Because of this, I conjectured for him that this track meet in front of him was possibly the greatest gift he could have. I described it as the perfect preparation for what was to come. I suggested that he embrace the pressure and be thankful for the chance to put his foot on the line and feel the heat.

I shared a perspective with him that I had developed from listening to the way champions think on game day:

> "I like to put myself in position where I feel like I'm choking my guts out, so that I can see how good I can become. You see other people running from pressure. My whole purpose is to put my foot on the line each day and feel the heat because where I intend to go is a place of fire."

I asked him if he ever thought like that. I suggested that his competitors did, and that he needed to embrace this quote and head to the meet looking forward to embracing the pressure.

In his report following the meet, Scott shared with me that he missed his first two attempts at a low bar. He had one attempt left and if he missed it, he would no-height in the meet and be seen as a failure to all the fans, coaches, and athletes watching. As he stood on the runway, he said he was angry, frustrated, and embarrassed as the fans watched. He then remembered the quote and said if the quote is true, he was about to jump 19 feet because he had never felt this much pressure. He took off down the runway, embracing the pressure, and he cleared the bar by two feet. Scott continued embracing the pressure for the remainder of the night. At his nemesis meet he didn't miss another height, and he became a national champion.

One year later at the outdoor national championship, Scott shattered the American record at 19 feet 7.25 inches. He was on his way to a great run up to the Olympics. But he had one more hurdle to clear. In the fall before the Olympic year, he pulled a muscle so badly in his thigh that he splintered his pelvic bone. This is an excruciating injury requiring a long recovery. He was not able to jump again in competition until right before the Olympic trials the following summer. Have you ever said, "Why me; why now?" Scott's injury couldn't have come at a worse time, but he embraced the pressure, knowing very well that his career might be over.

Scott showed up to the Olympic trials where they were staging the events just as they would be at the Olympic Games. The bus they put him on to the stadium broke down. Insult added to injury. He arrived late but just in time to take a few run-throughs to warm up. He missed two early attempts in a row and had to dig deep and embrace the pressure. He made the final attempt at his opening height and continued the fight for his Olympic dream. On his final attempt of the day, he secured the final spot on the Olympic vaulting team. Today, many years later, he still points to his turning point—the moment when he made the choice to embrace the pressure at his nemesis meet.

Scott indeed had to go through the fire to reach his dream. It was inspiring to watch. But there is more. I'll share other aspects of his incredible story in later chapters.

Where specifically do you need to embrace the pressure? In so doing how will this strengthen your mental toughness for the goals you have set?

CHAPTER 14

PRACTICE FOR THE EMERGENCIES

Knowing your response ahead of the situation, especially if it is an unexpected challenge, is critical to success.

I remember our motto in Boy Scouts, "Be Prepared," was so important to my mental toughness training. But the best lesson I ever received for being prepared was from my pilot instructor.

One of my life goals was to become a pilot. At 18 I went up with my first instructor. It was a beautiful October day with no thermals buffeting us around. It was like water skiing on a clear, glassy lake. At 2,000 feet he was teaching me how to maneuver the plane with the rudder and steering column. I had taken control of the plane for about five minutes when, unbeknownst to me, he turned the engine off. He declared that we had an emergency and needed to find a place immediately to land the plane because we didn't have time or altitude to reach the runway.

The instructor began to bark out orders, "Keep the nose down! Keep the wings level! Find a place to land!" while shoving the steering column forward and putting us into a deep dive. First, I chose a road that he nixed because of cars and power lines. Next, I chose a field which he overruled because of cows. Then I chose a cornfield, and he had the audacity to ask as the stall warning was beeping, "You landing with or against the rows?" I was not answering quickly enough, so he added, "With the rows so we don't flip the plane."

Nearing 500 feet he reached down, turned the engine on, and took control of the plane. After he took us back up to altitude, he made this profound statement: "Son, by law I cannot and will not sign you off to fly a plane by yourself or with passengers until you are prepared for the emergencies of flight. For the next 40 hours, if you would like to continue your flight training, we are going to prepare for every conceivable emergency that you might someday face until I believe you are prepared to land this plane in spite of them."

And that is exactly what we did. I remember the foundational strategy for being hit by a cross wind while landing: level the wings, full power, turn into the wind. This one saved me on several occasions. It was an automatic response that outweighed the fear of the moment.

At the end of the 40 hours of training, I was not afraid of an emergency. I was confident in my ability to handle it. By practicing for the emergencies, mental toughness was being established.

Preparing for emergencies is as easy as looking back at the past and seeing where you gave away a piece of your performance potential. Recall the setting and situation and determine the elements that stole your talent. Determine a specific strategy for attacking that emergency in the future. Write it down, rehearse it in your mind, and if possible, recreate the situation in order to scrimmage against it.

Another way to prepare is by observing others who failed and putting yourself in their place with a specific plan for winning the inner game. Confidence comes from being prepared.

Captain "Sully" Sullenberger took off from New York on January 15, 2009, not knowing that his passenger jet would hit a flock of birds at approximately 2,000 feet. He lost both engines over Manhattan. Sullenberger had about 20 seconds to make a decision of where to put down the plane with 155 people on board. He determined immediately that returning to the airport was out of the question and landing on the Hudson River was the only option. Miraculously, he landed US Airways Flight 1549 on the Hudson between two bridges, and every passenger on the plane survived. Later he said, "Every minute of my career as a pilot was preparation for that one moment."

Recently my wife was at Whole Foods and started a conversation with a woman, Karin Rooney, who had three young children in tow. The women quickly became friends and walked to a park next door where they could continue visiting as the children played. In the course of the conversation, Karin said she had recently authored a book, *Sink or Swim: Life After Crash Landing in the Hudson*. She said, "I was on US Airways Flight 1549." She was alive because her pilot had practiced for the emergencies and acted in a fearless manner. That puts it all in perspective.

I find it strange that golfers think hitting dozens of 5 irons on a perfectly manicured flat driving range to targets with no other ramifications is somehow preparation for what they will face on the golf course. The golf course seldom has a level lie and there are hazards lurking everywhere. Golf just may be the worst practiced sport in the world. Not many golfers prepare for the true emergencies of the game: wind effect, grass length effect, unlevel lie effect, elevation effect, grain, situational factors within the round, distractions, etc.

The evening before my first district tournament as a high school golfer, my dad and I found a grouping of trees from which to hit specialty shots with our shag balls as the sun was setting. My dad had me hit low punch shots under limbs, curving the ball around the trees, hitting high shots over the trees, and practicing bad lies in various lengths of grass while hitting these shots. I left that practice session knowing that at least I had a clue as to how to hit each shot. I won my first district tournament the following day. I owe that victory to my father's wise insight into my final "emergency" preparation for that event.

I often have executive teams share both their best practices and their toughest situations from the previous year. The strategic planning for overcoming performance debilitating situations from the previous year gives the group the greatest confidence, spark, and hope for succeeding in the upcoming year. While the same situations may not occur again, the idea of emergency training changes the game and frees the team.

As I think again about the recent groundbreaking brain research that seems to indicate the brain wasn't built for perfection but for adapting, what we really should be training are mentally tough adapters, not perfectionistic performers. In other words, emergencies will be a part of the landscape because perfection is unlikely going to define the environment in which we perform. Therefore, performing to the top of our capabilities while adapting to imperfections (emergencies) in the environment, in ourselves, and in the people with whom we interact is a champion's blueprint for success and a cornerstone to mental toughness.

What specific application can you take from this chapter? Apply it directly to several situations for which you have to be prepared.

CHAPTER 15

PAINT A MASTERPIECE

The pictures we paint with our mind's eye will greatly affect the outcome of performance—choose to paint a masterpiece.

Before and during every performance, we have a volitional choice of seeing success or seeing failure. The picture you choose will significantly affect the outcome. Your mind and body will work best when you are free. The picture you choose will determine the level of freedom within your body.

When I was 14, a mentor showed up at my little blue-collar golf course in Waco, Texas. His name was Johnny Arreaga. He was the man who introduced me to the mental game long before anyone was writing or talking about it.

One day while playing I noticed that every time Johnny hit a shot, he said "Picasso" as he replaced his club in his bag. He was on his way to shooting a 61 one particular day when I asked him why he always said Picasso after a shot. He had just replaced his 8 iron in his bag on this par three where he had hit it in there about three feet from the pin.

He said, "Come here, Cookie." As we stood on the tee box, he said, "Look out there and tell me what you see." I pointed out all the trouble—lake right, bunker short, false front, weeds to the left.

"You don't get it, do you?" he countered.

"I guess not," I replied, "but I'd like to know what you're wanting me to see."

He then began to give me my first sport psychology lesson years before there was a recognized field of study for it. "You have a blank canvas in front of you. Before each shot you have a choice to paint a picture. You can paint success or failure. It's your choice. I choose to paint a masterpiece before every shot. I create the shot I want to hit; not the shot I fear. And after I hit the shot, I simply sign the painting 'Picasso' as I put the club in my bag."

What a lesson. Johnny even verbalized "Picasso" as an accountability process for what he believed to be true.

Johnny has since died. At his funeral many years ago, Picasso was the common theme shared by those who spoke about how he lived life and the way he performed. Who would have foreseen that Academy Award winner Robert Duvall would play the part of Johnny in the movie *Seven Days in Utopia* that I would write and serve on as executive producer almost 40 years later?

About 20 years after my lesson from Johnny, I was with a PGA Tour player named Steve Lowery for the

International PGA Tour event at Castle Pines, Colorado. I alluded to this story earlier; here is the rest of the story.

As I mentioned Steve had just come off five missed cuts in a row. He was not in a good mood. Along the way he had drifted from his true identity as a player and was lost in a sea of mechanical thoughts—very technical aspects of the swing rather than allowing instinct to lead. I asked him to return to true north—his instincts, feel, and creativity. To get him there, I asked him to give his caddie permission not to give him a club unless he first "called his shot" by describing target, shape, and trajectory in detail. In essence, I was asking him to paint a masterpiece and to be accountable to the process to his caddie. He agreed.

It was amazing to see what happened during the practice round. He was a different person. He became free and began to play golf to the pictures he created. On the ninth hole during the practice round, the caddie said that this would be the playoff hole on Sunday if a sudden death playoff were required to determine the winner. So, I asked Steve what he would do if he were in a playoff. His first response was that he had missed five cuts in a row and being in a playoff was highly unlikely. I asked him why he was at the tournament. He said to win. I reminded him that PGA tournaments go to sudden death about 30 percent of the time. I told him that he didn't want to wait until Sunday afternoon under the chaos of the moment in sudden death to determine his strategy.

I suggested that he choose his shot now by painting a masterpiece.

He agreed and described a beautiful and detailed shot to his caddie, and then pulled it off. He looked at us both and said, "That's what I'll do on Sunday if I'm in a playoff."

Going into the 17th hole on Sunday afternoon, Steve needed a miracle to get into the playoff. As his second shot on this par five was rocketing to the hole, his caddie uttered one of the great caddie lines of all time heard on television, "If that ain't no good, there ain't no good!"

The ball landed next to the hole for a tap in eagle and the miracle he needed. With a subsequent par on 18, he was in the playoff with another young tour player who hadn't won. Steve picked number one out of the official's cap, and teed off first. He called his shot, painted his masterpiece out loud to his caddie, then ripped a perfect shot into the center of the fairway. His opponent walked into his shot, but backed off right before he took the club back and started the process over. The commentators were asking, "What is he thinking?" They knew something wasn't right.

The player walked back into his shot and proceeded to hit it in the water to the right. The commentator down on the course observed, "That was the same shot he hit on this hole earlier today or he would have already outright won this tournament."

Two players were trying to walk into their destiny and earn their first victory. They were the two best players in the world that day. On the playoff hole Steve was painting a masterpiece; he was committed to the process that he had visualized during the practice round, thus he had also practiced for the emergency. The other player was trying to block out a picture of disaster. When you try to block out the picture, it only gets bigger. Try saying "Don't think about a lemon" five times in a row without the image of the lemon gaining strength. However, if you tell yourself not to think about a lemon one time, then tell yourself to replace the lemon with an orange, the lemon is gone.

What the other golfer failed to know at that moment was how blocking an image wasn't the answer. Instead he needed to replace the negative picture with a masterpiece. It cost him dearly. He didn't want to fail. He was just missing a piece of information needed to pull off a victory when emotional chaos was raining down.

I find it interesting that I learned that lesson first with a blue-collar golf pro when I was a young aspiring player, then had it confirmed in my doctoral training and research, and I finally shared it with a player who was in desperate need of a mental overhaul at the lowest point of his career. The principle of painting a masterpiece changed his life and brought him a victory out of the ashes. What an amazing journey I saw from my vantage point.

What specific application can you make from these stories to your life today? What does your blank canvas look like that looms in front of you? Take a few minutes and paint a masterpiece with your words. Put it on your mirror or wherever you can see it each day. Update it, live for it, believe in it.

CHAPTER 16

Trust Your Talent

Trust is a volitional decision to believe made at a moment in time.

Trust is a powerful word. When you trust, you are free and confident. Your mind and body have a chance to work with precision. Trust is a decision made at a moment in time to believe in your training, education, experience, ability, and talent. It is a decision to believe in the masterpiece you painted to solve the emergencies for which you have practiced. It isn't based on stats or recent performance. It is simply a choice to believe in your talent. It is a volitional statement that says, "I will trust."

A few years back I was asked to work with the number one Division I collegiate women's volleyball team in the nation. Their coach, Terry Petit, had a 21-year mission of bringing a national championship to this school. That year they were in position for it to happen. They went 34-1 and had one match left. It was the national championship match. A few days before that match coach called, concerned. Who wouldn't be? He was facing the goal of his life and playing a formidable team. He was a brilliant coach who really didn't need me, but he trusted me and his assistants greatly and often used us as sounding boards. His thought was this: He had four All-Americans on the court, and another who would be All-American the following year. His sixth girl was Kate. She was an outside hitter and a really good athlete, but compared to the others, she was the weak link on the court. The coach knew the other team would try to exploit her. He loved Kate, but she was just a little unorthodox in how she played. They had worked hard on her skills during the year.

He wondered out loud to me if he should replace her and start the game with an outstanding freshman who had come on strong during the season. Like most of us with time to think and a huge goal on the line, his mind raced forward to think of ways to correct imperfections at the last minute.

We discussed the options—starting a freshman in the national championship match for the first start of her life or leaving Kate in. My main concern that I expressed to him was that game day was about trust and sowing seeds of trust with the team. I explained to him there was a real possibility of undermining trust with the other five girls on the court if he made a drastic change at the last minute. They might think, "He must not think we're ready or good enough. Look what he's doing."

I suggested the best option for establishing trust across the board was to speak greatness over Kate and let her know that he believed in her, that he trusted her, that he was proud of her. I thought it was important for him to free her mind and tell her to have fun and just play the game. Tell her that she was ready and prepared. I also encouraged him to go beyond Kate and to instill trust in each of his players and speak greatness over each one independently before the match. Trust was his mission for the match.

He did just that. He spoke greatness over Kate and the other girls. Kate had averaged about five or so kills per match for the year. In the national championship match, Kate had 25 kills and 21 digs to go with it. She was named MVP of the match and was named to the all-tournament team. The girl he was contemplating taking out set an NCAA record for the most kills in an NCAA playoff game.

Later during the celebration, the coach spoke with Kate. He looked her in the eye and said, "Kate you were special today! No one has ever done what you just did. What was the difference?" She stopped the tears just long enough to look back in his eyes and say, "Coach, it's the first time you really trusted in me."

At that moment this favorite coach of mine knew the truth. He knew that his words had changed Kate's destiny. He knew from that moment on, he would consider sacred the words that he'd use with his team, his wife, his daughter, and his friends. He knew his words would give life or take life from the hearts of those with whom he interacted. The word *trust* was powerful—powerful enough to bring home the national championship trophy.

I was the director of Applied Sport Psychology at the University of Kansas many years ago when Roy Williams was introduced as our new head basketball coach (before his tenure at North Carolina). He had never been a head coach and was a relative unknown at that time to have received one of the premier college basketball jobs in the country. After a 16-2 start everyone was firmly on board. Then they lost five games in a row. The losses were mainly due to our main shooter and best player going from shooting 50 percent for the first 17 games to shooting about 20 percent during those five games. His name was Milt Newton and to this day he is still one of my all-time favorite athletes and human beings. Roy sent him over to see me before we were to play the number one team in the nation in our home arena.

I asked Milt what was going on, and he said he had lost his shot. I asked him what his strengths as a player were. He said he had always been a great shooter. I asked when he had become a bad shooter, and he replied, "A couple weeks ago." He was a 50 percent shooter for life and was in a two-week slump that looked like the end of the world for him and the fans. I asked him to remember back to when he shot well and recall what he thought. He said he just trusted it. I asked what he was thinking now, and he said he was thinking about how he was letting his team, coaches, and fans down. He showed me a line in the school newspaper that said, "As goes Milt's shooting, so go the Jayhawks!" He said he was also receiving lots of mechanical advice, including a letter from a lady in western Kansas who said he needed to wave at the basket with his follow-through.

I discussed the power of trust and gave him an assignment to write a script about one page in length that described his pre-game mental preparation along with creating a masterpiece vision for the game, emphasizing the word *trust*. I then asked him to record himself reading his "trust script" with music of his choice in the background. This become his mastery script for the game.

Milt did a great job of writing out a script of trusting his shot, his training, his ability, his talent, and other things that mattered to him. He included pre-game thoughts and mental prep along with some visualization of the game. The word *trust* was in just about every sentence. I asked him to listen to the recording as many times as possible before the game the following day.

He shot 56 percent in the game against the number one team in the nation and scored over 25 points. We lost in triple overtime, but it was one of the games of his life.

He came in to see me the day after the game, excited to make another script as they were playing Duke, ranked in the top five. He wrote a new script, recorded it over music, listened to it over and over, and again he shot above 50 percent and scored more than 20 points. However, we lost in double overtime.

Milt made a trust script with me for the final seven games including another top five team that we beat. We won all but the two overtime games, and Milt scored 20 points or more in each.

The final game was the most rewarding. He was sick and shooting 45 percent for the game in a very difficult and loud arena. There were five seconds on the clock and we were down by two but had the ball. Coach called for a play. The ball went in to Milt at the top of the key. It looked like he was heading for the basket to try to tie the game or get fouled. After a head fake and two initial steps, he stopped dead in his tracks, backed up two steps outside the three-point line and let a three-point shot fly. The Kansas fans, few and far between, yelled, "No, no, no … Yes!!!" as the ball swished through the net. We won by one.

The next day I asked Milt what he was thinking when he shot the three. He gave me the greatest answer I have ever gotten from a performer. He simply said, "I was just playing basketball." Wow, how profound. When I met him, he was trying to avoid failure. With the trust scripts, he was able to transition back to playing the game. Isn't that what you want … just to do your job well with trust?

And finally, back to Scott, the world-class vaulter I spoke about a few chapters back. I was working with him earlier in his career when he had fallen into a huge slump. He had jumped over 18 feet about 15 times in college. Now that he had graduated, gotten married, and was competing as a professional, he hadn't jumped over 17 feet 3 inches for eight months. His coach called and said Scott was testing better than ever in each of the 10 vaulting drills. "But," he said, "he just can't put it all together."

When Scott came to see me, I could tell there was a lot of weight on his shoulders. He felt the pressure of being a husband and not making any money. He wasn't being invited to any meets since he hadn't jumped 18 feet for a while. He felt like he was letting his coach down, and he was frustrated by not meeting his own expectations.

I asked him to do something: to write a letter to his best friend. He thought that was a curious task. I told him he needed to write an audacity letter to himself. He needed to return to being his own best friend again. I wanted him to write a letter to himself explaining why he ever had the audacity to think he could become a professional track athlete and possibly go to the Olympics one day, an audacious goal for sure. I wanted to see if he could return to a greatness mindset, a place he had lived for so long. He had previously lived there because he trusted himself and his dreams. I needed him to dig deep and tell himself why he allowed himself to dream the dream of greatness.

Scott took the task seriously and wrote an amazing and deep letter, speaking greatness over himself. He spoke of his tremendous speed and strength as a vaulter. He spoke of his many victories and records. He spoke of his training and preparation under the world's greatest coach. The letter was multiple pages and heartfelt.

I asked Scott if he believed what he wrote, and he said he did. It was literally his trust letter. He left my office that day with a new resolve.

That weekend he jumped as an independent in an all-comers meet and cleared 18 feet for the first time in nearly nine months. This earned him an invitation into a professional meet in New York City the following week, where he jumped 18 feet 4 inches and finished third. He flew to Los Angeles the next week for a big meet and jumped 18 feet 8 inches to win. He flew back to New York and jumped 17 feet 11 inches and placed in the top five. He went to Europe for a meet the following week and jumped 18 feet 4 inches. He returned to the states the next week and jumped 19 feet 2 inches—the third person in the United States to jump over 19 feet! The six weeks following the writing of Scott's audacity letter were magical for him. His trust was restored, and his professional career was off and running.

What are the talents and gifts and abilities you possess that have been shut down by doubt? What do you need to do right now in your mind to release the truth, quit focusing on the lies, and trust yourself going forward?

CHAPTER 17

PERSEVERE

Perseverance is an act of your will against logic and common sense.

Perseverance. The word really says it all. We all have been there. Nothing seems like it's working, and the slump continues. Discouragement envelops every pore of your body. No light shines at the end of the tunnel. The tunnel has collapsed. Perseverance becomes an act of your will against logic and common sense. Against all odds you summon the strength to take one more step.

Pat Manson was an amazing athlete and student. He was a very disciplined and coachable athlete. It was the Olympic year. His best friend and training partner, Scott, the vaulter I just described in the previous chapter, was injured. During this time Pat was surging during the indoor season. He was leading the Grand Prix series for professional track and field for the vault. The winner of the series, which included the entire indoor season, would receive a huge cash bonus. The series was set to culminate in a few weeks at the national indoor championship.

Pat showed up at my office asking if we could talk. He looked troubled. I congratulated him on his consistent top five performances each week that had him leading the Grand Prix.

Then I asked what was troubling him. His response was telling. He said he was having a good season, finishing high each week. But he said finishing high wasn't his goal. He wanted to win, and he hadn't won a big meet. He said he had a little hold back in his game which helped him with consistency, but it held him back from knowing just how high he could jump. He basically was saying he had risk aversion. He wanted to know how to let it go, how to find out what his true potential was—to take a risk.

For the next few weeks we met and discussed everything I've covered in this book up to this point. I asked him to write about each concept and expound how each was relevant to his situation. He was committed.

A few weeks into it was the final week, the week of the national championship. This was our targeted meet for him to compete on a new plane, letting it all go. Our final meeting was to be on Wednesday at 10 a.m. Our final topic would be perseverance. However, tragedy struck. As Pat was attempting a practice vault late in the day on Tuesday, his fiberglass pole broke. The bottom portion caught him between the eyes and slashed his face and scalp all the way to the bone from his forehead to the back of his head. He was rushed unconscious to the hospital by the EMS. He had lost a lot of blood and had possibly broken his neck or back. He was going into shock so they air transported him to a trauma center in nearby Kansas City.

I didn't hear about the accident until Wednesday morning at my 9 o'clock class where one of the track athletes let me know. I finished the class early and canceled all my appointments in an effort to get to the hospital. I was about to rush out of my office when there was a knock on my door. I opened it to see an almost unrecognizable young man. He had a turban of gauze around his head; his eyes were nearly swollen shut. It was Pat, keeping our 10 o'clock appointment.

He came in and told me the story. He said he suffered no broken bones and only a slight concussion (this was back before concussion protocol). He said the doctor tied his head together with "rope" that included 32 stitches.

I asked why he was smiling. He explained that he had a plan. He wanted to go to the meet with 32 stitches in his head, win the national championship, and be able to tell the story of how the things we had been talking about really worked. I was wondering about a waiver at that point!

Pat added that the doctor told him the stitches wouldn't break, the swelling would go down in a day, and that he could use Advil for the pain. Pat said he planned not to take any warm-up jumps and just wait until the bar got up around 18 feet, then he would enter and win with just a few vaults. I let him share the plan, knowing that the chances of his being cleared by his parents, doctors, and meet directors would be nearly insurmountable.

But guess what? Pat persevered. He persuaded them all to let him try it. At 18 feet he entered the event looking a little like Frankenstein. He made it on his first attempt as he did the next height. It came down to one other competitor and Pat. The bar was set at his personal record (PR) and the stadium and meet record of 18 feet 8.25 inches. With the crowd behind him he made it on his first attempt! His competitor made it on his third attempt. The bar was raised to a new PR, a new stadium record, a new meet record of 18 feet 11.25 inches. On Pat's first attempt he made it. His competitor missed his three attempts. Pat won the national championship with 32 stitches in his head.

How was that humanly possible? The tunnel had caved in … there was no light. Pat chose not to lie in the hospital bed while his dream chance for greatness passed him by. He took a step, then another, then he made a plan. He persevered. We never got to talk about perseverance. He just lived it.

Are there some steps in your life right now that are requiring you to persevere? Name them. Make a decision to take another step, and then another, then another … greatness could be a few steps away.

PILLAR IV:
SELFLESSNESS

"Do your words and actions reflect a noble heart that inspires greatness in others and makes those around you better?"

If your goal in life is exceptionalism (being successful, being a champion), then your pursuit is done. Apply the three pillars described in the previous chapters and you will perform as never before. But if one or more of the statements below is true about you, read on …

If you win but still feel empty, read on …

If you feel burned out by the never-ending performance chase, read on …

If the allure of success has stolen too many moments from your personal life, read on …

If the scoreboard and the opinions of others have defined your self-worth, read on …

If the fear of failure is always hounding you, read on …

If you want to move from success to significance, read on …

If success has led to isolation at the top, read on …

If success has given you fear-based power over those around you, read on …

greatness is a page away…

CHAPTER 18
Selfless Exceptionalism

We started this book by revealing that the greatest predictors of success or exceptionalism were focus, passion, and mental toughness, defined by the three questions below. These also serve as the first three pillars to greatness:

1. Where do you want to go? (Focus)
2. How bad do you want to reach your goal? (Passion)
3. Do you have the mental skills needed to handle the adversity along the way? (Mental toughness)

The fourth and defining pillar of greatness is choosing selflessness. It affects how you answer this defining question:

4. Do your words and actions reflect a noble heart that inspires greatness in others and makes those around you better?

Greatness is defined as selfless exceptionalism. Choosing a selfless heart is the defining pillar of greatness. It is a place of exceptional performances for the purpose of enhancing and encouraging the lives of others.

When you choose greatness, you perform to inspire and encourage, you lead to inspire and encourage, you choose exceptionalism to inspire and encourage, your life mission is to make the lives of those around you—your team, community, nation, and world—better during the journey. Victory is defined more by the positive effect you have on others versus the trophy or accolades or personal gain you may receive. Inspiring others to greatness is the greatest legacy you can leave to the world.

Greatness doesn't bask in the limelight. It redirects it to others. Greatness isn't about being larger than life or the center of the universe. It's about being a servant, a giver. It isn't about *me*. It's about others. Greatness goes through success and then keeps going. Greatness is the place beyond success. Not all champions reach this mark: only those with a noble heart; only those with a selfless ego.

Two major traits radiate from people of greatness: the need to achieve and the need to give.

Greatness people combine these creatively to do things very few have ever achieved, while at the same time using the journey and the achievements to change the world around them. Their legacy is powerful yet *other-focused*. Those of true greatness lift others, encourage others, and inspire others with their words and exceptional actions. They call out and guard the dreams of others. They are dream guardians. They live above the negative stereotypes associated with limelight-seeking champions: greed, anger, selfishness, intimidation, and rule bending. Their character is to give, not take.

CHAPTER 19

NOBLE HEART

When you give you live; when you take you ache.
Those who give are marked with a noble heart.

Viktor Frankl, in his groundbreaking book *Man's Search for Meaning*, addressed *giving* in a roundabout way. He studied people imprisoned in the worst imaginable circumstances during World War II. The German concentration camps stripped people of all human dignity and reason to live. Yet he observed that some lived and some died. Was there an ultimate reason that separated the two? His conclusion, in my words, was "When you give you live." Frankl discovered that those who gave of themselves to help others, even when they were weak, feeble, and sick, lived longer than those who spiraled downward and became inwardly focused. If that is the case in a dire life-and-death situation, it certainly is applicable to our daily lives.

During my second year with the Spurs, I had a front row seat to greatness unfolding. I was in Aspen sitting under a pine tree with a trout stream to my right and an outdoor basketball court to my left. The world was passing by as if nothing special were happening. But I knew differently. To a discerning trout enthusiast, I knew this was a blue-ribbon trout haven that fishermen dream about; and on the court were two young men who would one day both earn their way into the NBA

Hall of Fame. Furthermore, they would win several NBA championships and both earn the coveted NBA MVP award. But on this day, something deeper was transpiring. Greatness was on display.

David Robinson and Tim Duncan were meeting for the first time, and they did it in a casual game of one on one. I was the only spectator, invited by David, but sitting at a distance so as not to distract from the focus of the meeting. Upon Tim's being drafted by the team, David invited him to his summer home in Aspen to get to know him and make him feel welcome.

What was happening was the transfer of greatness from one man to another. Tim was unaware that David was strategically anointing him as the eventual new leader of the team. While it would take several years for that succession process to take hold, David opened the door with an astounding display of selflessness. In his mind the bigger picture was how could he provide an atmosphere in which Tim would thrive. In other words, how could David use his goals, influence, experience, and mentoring to make his teammate a better player and a better man?

It was a noble heart that fueled David's passion across the next seven years which included the Spurs' first two world championships. David played with uncanny freedom and joy because he was a giver, not a taker. And Tim thrived because he knew that he wasn't seen as a threat but a true teammate and friend. David modeled selfless exceptionalism when he chose a noble heart.

This mentoring of greatness also transferred. A number of years later when a major hurricane hit the islands where Tim was raised, he immediately got involved. Not only did he provide financially for his community, but he also showed up in person and physically worked tirelessly helping the people put their lives and island back together. He got in the dirt. He gave. When you give you live.

I wrote in several earlier chapters about Scott, the Olympic pole-vaulter. Here is the rest of his compelling story. It was the day of the Olympic trials, the biggest competitive day of his life. His best friend Pat, Scott's former collegiate teammate, was also competing. Pat was the vaulter who had just won the indoor national championship with 32 stitches in his head.

On Pat's first warm-up jump at the Olympic trials, his pole broke again. This time it missed his head. He careened out of control through the vaulting pit, eventually ending up on the ground. After he dusted himself off and caught his breath, he took a look at his other back-up poles. A faint tire tread mark showed across them. It appeared that a baggage handler at the airport had accidentally run over his poles, compromising them all.

What in the world was he going to do? He knew one other competitor in the event with similar poles: Scott. Pat thought about his dilemma carefully while the medical staff checked him out. Asking Scott if he could borrow his poles would be adding more interference to his friend who had already had his share of major interference, including the fact he was stuck on a broken-down bus somewhere.

In the end Pat decided to ask. Scott immediately, graciously, and enthusiastically said yes. He said yes knowing that he and Pat prepared their pole grips very differently before each jump and this would be another significant interference to performing on such a pressurized stage. Brotherhood and friendship meant more to Scott than the extra pressure of sharing the same pole. He invited in the interference and embraced it. Scott was a giver. He chose to have a noble heart.

When the announcer came on the speaker later in the day, the audience had no idea what had transpired during the warm up. The announcer said, "If we can have your attention in the pole vault area, Pat Manson is preparing for his final attempt in the vault. If he makes it, he will be the final competitor to make the pole vaulting team for the Olympics." Pat was using Scott's pole. If he missed, Scott would receive the final spot on the team. It came down to this one jump on a borrowed pole.

Pat barely missed the attempt, and Scott earned the final spot. I share this story because of its significance to greatness. Scott displayed greatness by being willing to give away his ultimate sport dream so that Pat would have a chance at that same dream. He shared his poles. He cared more about his friend at that moment than about himself. Scott is the model of greatness—selfless exceptionalism.

In 1996 Tom Lehman and Steve Jones were tied going into the final hole of the US Open. Steve was noticeably anxious as he moved from the 17th green to the 18th tee box. Observing this, Tom reached out and quoted a calming scripture for his friend and competitor as they walked to the tee box. Jones responded with thanks. He calmed down, focused, and parred the final hole, while Lehman unfortunately slipped to a bogie. Steve Jones won the US Open with the encouragement of Tom who reached out "inside the ropes" and willingly gave life-giving words to his competitor. Tom has a noble heart. Though Tom failed to win that major, he won his major at the British Open one month later. Tom Lehman is a man of greatness.

I'm not sure I have been more affected by any story I have been involved with than this next one. As I mentioned in a powerful story of trust earlier in the book, Terry Pettit was the women's volleyball coach at the University of Nebraska. In 1995 he invited me to join them as they set their goal and sights on a national championship. During my service to him and his team that year we had many deep talks. On one occasion I asked if he coached out of unconditional love or conditional love based on performance. That is a deep question for a coach at that level. While everything is judged by the scoreboard, the parents of these young women had entrusted their greatest gifts to the coach. Unconditional love doesn't mean a coach isn't demanding or driving or tough, it just means that at the end of the day, his or her team knows they are loved. He told me that he wanted to think about it and would get back to me with the answer.

His answer came in action during the semifinal match of the NCAA national championship volleyball tournament. In the final game of the match, they were tied 7-7 in a very emotional and heated match. Everything was on the line. Only one team was going to advance to the finals. The opposition was on a roll. A TV time-out was signaled. Coach approached the huddle not knowing exactly what he was going to say. He could sense the intensity in the air. The momentum had shifted to the opponent.

As his players gathered around, he shocked them by giving them no technical advice or instruction or special play. Instead, he looked at each one of them slowly and deeply, then said, "No matter if we win or lose, you need to know something." He paused, choking back tears, and then continued, "I love you each very, very much." And with that he continued to look around at each of them, making it personal, then he simply retreated to the bench, leaving them stunned but forever changed. What he said released them to play fearlessly and freely. They shocked their opponent by scoring eight of the next nine points to win the match. It was an awe-inspiring reversal of momentum. Coach Petit displayed a noble heart. They won their first-ever national championship trophy in the next match. The fearlessness continued. Terry is a man of greatness.

A noble heart intensifies desire because in the end it is a win for more than self. It spills out to the team, the organization, family, friends, society, or others it touches. It leaves a lasting legacy. Because it is other-focused, there is less of a chance to spiral down into selfishness that would ultimately lead to emptiness and lack of fulfillment. Greatness, unlike success alone, leads to fulfillment. In the end, fulfillment is the longing of every person's heart. It is found in the place beyond success. It is called greatness, and only those with noble hearts can enter.

I wrote a couple of novels about greatness before penning this book: *Seven Days in Utopia: Golf's Sacred Journey* and *Golf's Sacred Journey, The Sequel*. You can find them at linksofutopia.com. I invite you to explore this concept more deeply in these two novels. You will find a story of a young performer searching for success but finding greatness in the end. These two books are an imperative next step in your journey. Please don't stop now.

CHAPTER 20

YOUR PERSONAL GREATNESS LETTER

Psychologists tell us that the most intimate and influential messages we will ever receive in life come from what we say to ourselves, not what others say to us. I have seen this truth change the lives of many, especially those who have had false and debilitating labels hung around their necks from others. It's time to find your noble heart and dream big dreams. These dreams will emanate from within. Listen to your heart. Take the time to write a letter to yourself using the guidelines from this book.

In your personal letter of greatness, start by discussing your noble goals. Describe specifically how the pursuit of those goals will enhance the lives of those around you during the chase and also at the trophy celebration one day. Make these goals specific, tangible, difficult, and self-referenced. Discuss your great passion for a life of fulfillment that fuels these goals. Include ideas about ownership, accountability, incentive, and fun. And finally, in your letter commit to incorporating the tools of mental toughness that will serve you along the way: embracing the pressure, practicing for the emergencies, painting a masterpiece, trusting your training and talent, and persevering.

Make your letter about two pages in length and read it often. A shorter letter makes this effort more practical.

Read it before games or critical business meetings, during rehab, after victories. Update it often as goals change and new words of encouragement emerge within you. Take this seriously and you will begin to hear a different voice while you are competing. You will hear your audacious words and they will lead your focus and emotions.

The world is in need of greatness. Find your noble heart and unleash it as you pursue your dreams. When you perform with a noble heart, you will become free. It is one of the deep secrets all performers are searching for. The problem for most of them: they fall one pillar short.

CHAPTER 21

THE FINAL FRONTIER

This chapter is sealed for a reason. I want you to take your time and think about it before you invest time in this chapter. The information you have read thus far is the best I have to offer in the professional sense. It is powerful and will change your performance life. This chapter, however, is my story. It is personal. It is an intimate look into the "locker room" of true fearlessness that unfortunately can't be found in the four pillars alone. It is the foundation upon which the four pillars rest. Pillars fall without a solid foundation.

It has been said that the mind is the final frontier to performance. It isn't. What is behind this seal is the final frontier. It holds the secret to fearless performance. It is a dangerous chapter to write … it is a dangerous chapter to read. It is dangerous because it speaks of a narrow road and the narrow road always ignites the fury of the naysayers—the gatekeepers of the broad road of conformity. Break the seal at your own risk, or skip to the Final Thoughts section and take what you have been given thus far and go change the world through your dreams and talents.

I have let you into the locker room, inside the ropes, and onto the sidelines in the previous chapters. I have always seen it as a privilege to be given access to that hallowed ground with those special performers. It is my prayer that those principles and stories will transform your performance. What I am about to share is more intimate and more important. This is about the foundation upon which my pillars rest. I am about to share the intimate details of my personal story. The world believes the final frontier is in the mind. I know better. The mind is the penultimate step. The final frontier is in the heart. In fact, the ancient words tell us the heart is the wellspring of life.

I have always believed that two are better than one. When facing the raging challenges of this life, we need an advocate. We need a voice of wisdom that is with us in the heat of the battle. We don't need that voice to be on the sidelines; we need it as close as possible, in our hearts.

Let me explain. The real dragon in this world is fear. The previous chapters help us hold the dragon at bay. But they have not eliminated the effects of fear, just managed it. Its roots have to be understood and destroyed if we are to become fearless, and fearless is what I am after, and I suspect you are as well because you broke the seal.

The seal is important. It is a symbol that you made an investment to seek something. I am thankful you have done that. It is my prayer that what I am about to reveal opens a new realm for you.

A moment arose in my life when I was sick of fear, sick of losing because of fear, and finished with the fear of failure hounding me at every aspect of sport, business, and my life in general. Fear is the underlying source of mental mistakes and meltdowns, anger, frustration, jealousy, envy, depression, oppression, hate, cheating, pride—everything that corrupts us. You name it and at the root is fear.

In my search, I discovered many ways to hold it at bay. In fact, I basically have a Ph.D. in holding fear at bay. But there is only one way to eradicate it. It is part of my story. It has to be shared.

I thought long and hard about sharing this. Ultimately, I realized that without it I would not have told you the entire truth, thus leaving you unprepared for all that is in front of you—all that you are called to do.

So here is the secret of fearlessness, the foundation for my four pillars:

I took God at His word.

Somewhere along my journey the words quoted below jumped off the pages of scripture. I had a choice to believe that they were true or that they were a myth. That God was real or not. I had a choice to take God at His word. My choice would ultimately revolutionize everything I did.

Here is what I read:

"Perfect love drives out fear."
                    (1 John 4:18 NIV)

A few sentences before this, John writes, "God is love." Putting the two together reveals the secret: "God drives out fear." Stay with me. The scriptures also make this truth clear through a very dramatic moment in Jesus' life the night he was betrayed and handed over for crucifixion. He told his followers this awe-inspiring revelation, maybe the most unbelievable words in the history of the world. He said that He had to go; in His mind He knew that meant to be killed in order that the Holy Spirit, God's voice to us, could come and live inside of us in our hearts. He called the Holy Spirit the counselor, the comforter, and the voice of all truth. This is the advocate I was looking for. And Jesus said this advocate would reside in your heart, not in your mind.

When you take God at His word and put all of this together, this is what you get. As a follower of Jesus you get an advocate on the inside, a voice that is with you, and that voice has a source. That source has the power to drive out fear. And that is the answer to being fearless in sport, business, and life.

Let me tell you about the great and mystical exchange. Again, it is awe inspiring and one of the most important principles in this new realm with God. The entire textbook on psychology written by God is contained in three verses of the entire Bible. Again, I took Him at His word. That is all you have to do. What God does in these three verses, Freud and others couldn't do in volumes and volumes of books on psychology.

> *"Do not be anxious [fearful] about anything, but in every situation, by prayer and petition, with thanksgiving, present your requests to God. And the peace of God, which transcends all understanding, will guard your hearts and your minds in Christ Jesus. Finally, brothers and sisters, whatever is true, whatever is noble, whatever is right, whatever is pure, whatever is lovely, whatever is admirable—if anything is excellent or praiseworthy—think about such things."*
> (Philippians 4:6-8 NIV)

Here is the key to a fearless performance—a fearless life. I call it the great exchange with God. He is holding out His hand to us, asking us to give Him the bad stuff (fear). He understands its debilitating effect on the human brain and heart. In His hand He is holding out the good stuff in return. Give your fears to God; He loves to take the weight. And in the big exchange, He replaces fear with peace, peace that surpasses our understanding. Then He leads our minds in a new direction—to think on these things—whatever is true, noble, right, pure, lovely, admirable, excellent, and praiseworthy. And when we do, we break the cycle of giving ground to fear again. But, by God's grace if we do become anxious or fearful again, we are human; we have this process to return to. And this process doesn't hold fear and anxiety at bay, it removes it—God gladly takes it—again and again and again, He takes it and removes it.

Let's put this all together. God is by nature love and love drives out fear—God drives out fear. Jesus said the Holy Spirit of God lives in us as followers of Jesus, and therefore we have at all times an advocate and that advocate is ready to drive out fear at any time we give it to His outstretched hand, replacing fear with peace, and peace opens the floodgates to reaching maximum potential.

When I simply took God at His word, He did the rest and continues to each day. I don't win every competition, earn every deal, write a best seller every time, say the right thing, or think the right way. But I have an advocate every moment encouraging me to listen to His wisdom in all situations, and when I do, I win even if the scoreboard shares a different story.

I spoke about SFT in this book. I call it the neural pathway to performance: see, feel, and trust. Let me add to it. See, feel, and trust is about the mind. Let's take it one step further, to the final frontier—the heart. Let's look at the deeper meaning of SFT to complete the neural pathway to fearlessness. Let's take God at His word and add this meaning as our reminder: *See* His face. *Feel* His presence. *Trust* His love. SFT.

When you give SFT both meanings, you are performing and living off a foundation of fearlessness with God in your heart, and you have a mental process for your mind as well for each performance moment of your life.

I wrote my first book about this belief. *Seven Days in Utopia: Golf's Sacred Journey* is "true fiction" if you will, that changes names and identities but tells the true story of how a person moves through the stages of greatness. The mentor leads the young performer on a journey of success to start with that transcends into significance when he eventually takes God at His word. If you have not read it, please take this opportunity to make the journey to Utopia through the pages of *Seven Days in Utopia*. Your life will never be the same. There is a sequel as well that will complete your journey to fearlessness.

You were meant for greatness. Take God at His word and follow the narrow road to the final frontier of the heart as you slay the dragon that has been holding you back. See His face; Feel His presence; Trust His love: SFT.

Add this new meaning of SFT to your greatness letter, make it foundational to each of the four pillars, and discover what fearless performance looks and feels like. You will be awestruck.

> "The greatest among you will be your servant. For those who exalt themselves will be humbled, and those who humble themselves will be exalted."
> (Matthew 23:11-12 NIV)

Final Thoughts

We have been born into a challenging world. Competition is fierce. Defining moments emerge unannounced. Do you know a person, organization, or team who has lost their dream along the way or had a setback? Do you know anyone who is about to embark on a new venture that will take all their skills and more? There may be someone within your sphere of influence who could use this message. I sent along a small easel for this purpose. It is often hard to create deep conversations with others. It is my hope that when you set this book on the easel and place it on your desk or shelf, that it will cause people to lean in out of curiosity to read the title and then ask, "What is that about," or "Why the small g?" My prayer is that it will spark many deep conversations about selfless exceptionalism with those searching for more in their lives.

Greatness is at work when we use our influence to enhance the lives of others. In our world today, a book given to a friend or colleague is a book that will be read and incorporated in their lives, especially one signed to them by you. Your gift to them is waiting at davidcookconsulting.com or linksofutopia.com.

About the Author

David L. Cook, Ph.D.

David Cook is a speaker, peak performance coach, author, and filmmaker in the field of Sport and Performance Psychology. He served as Mental Training Coach for the San Antonio Spurs from 1996 to 2004, a period that included two world championships. He has also held similar positions with the Washington Wizards, Houston Rockets, and Atlanta Hawks. *Golf Digest* (2013) named him one of the "Top 10 Mental Game Experts" in the world of golf. As past president of the National Sport Psychology Academy, David is known as a leading authority in the science of Peak Performance. He has coached players from the PGA, NBA (including two NBA MVPs, David Robinson and Tim Duncan), NFL, MLB, Olympics, and collegiate national championship ranks. His business clients have included Insperity, PGA of America, Exxon Mobil, Sprint, HP/Compaq, USAA, Heinz, Raytheon, Frito Lay, Whole Foods, Valero, Memorial Hermann Hospitals of Houston, American Express, Bristol-Myers Squibb, Texas Instruments, Bayer, Interstate Battery, StorageTek, Pitney Bowes, US Filter, State Farm Insurance, Robert Half International, Key Bank, Conoco/Phillips, and many others.

In 2006 David released his best-selling performance novel, *Golf's Sacred Journey: Seven Days at the Links of Utopia*, which was featured in the *USA Today* Life Section. This book was made into an award-winning movie, *Seven Days in Utopia*, with Academy Award winners Robert Duvall and Melissa Leo and was released in theaters across the country. The movie was built around the performance principles he teaches. He served as executive producer on this project and president and chairman of the board of Utopia Films, the production company. The book's sequel, *Golf's Sacred Journey: The Sequel*, was published in the spring of 2018.

David's Peak Performance consulting firm bridges the gap between the sports and business arenas. He is the former director of Applied Sport and Performance Psychology at the University of Kansas (1984-1996) where his peers elected him president of the National Sport Psychology Academy in 1992. During his 12-year tenure at KU, he counseled over 2,500 athletes and coaches and directed the graduate program in Applied Sport Psychology. David's articles have been featured in *Golf Magazine, Golf Illustrated*, and *Golf Tips*. In 1988 David represented the United States at the International Olympic Academy in Olympia, Greece.

David received his undergraduate degree from Baylor University in 1980. He completed his Ph.D. in Applied Sport and Performance Psychology from the University of Virginia in 1984. He is married to Karen and has two daughters. They live in the Hill Country of Texas.

For information regarding speaking, consulting, or to review David's other books and movie, go to the websites davidcookconsulting.com or linksofutopia.com.